Summary of Breath:

The New Science of a Lost Art

By James Nestor

Smart Reads

Note to readers:
This is an unofficial summary & analysis of
James Nestor's "Breath: The New Science of
a Lost Art" designed to enrich your reading
experience. The original book can be
purchased on Amazon.

Download Your Free Gift

As a way to say "Thank You" for being a fan of our series, I've included a free gift for you:

Brain Health: How to Nurture and Nourish Your Brain For Top Performance

Go to www.smart-reads.com to get your FREE book.

The Smart Reads Team

Table of Contents

Overview of *Breath: The New Science of a Lost Art*

Breath: The New Science of a Lost Art is a book by James Nestor, an author, and journalist whose proficiency and research made him discover the potency of breathing well. Something that modern Man has lost along the way. While science is only just finding out some of these secrets, the ancient text left to us by humans centuries and millennials ago has provided us with vast information on how breathing and enlarging your lung can extend your life spam and well-being.

The book's introduction talks about the author going for a breathing class that teaches the technique called *Sudarshan Kriya*. When the training started, he wasn't sure how to sit on the floor and breathe while a man with an Indian accent spoke to him from the speaker. The frustrating feeling soon dissolved as he noticed he felt very fine even though he was stressed and on the verge of breaking down before he arrived there. Breathing has always been an essential part of our existence, but none took this seriously as the ancient Chinese who wrote about seven books going back over 400 BCE about breathing. And, judging from how well and long they live, what they have to say shouldn't be ignored. Surprisingly, many of the things written in Tibetans, Hindus, and Chinese texts are backed by science. It only arouses the curiosity of the author more. This fuelled his research and soon he began to have first-hand experience of how helpful breathing well can be. On average, humans will take about 670 million breaths, so it's best to make this count.

Chapter 1: The Worst Breathers in the Animal Kingdom

Chapter one of Breath: *The New Science of A Lost Art* is titled The Worst Breathers in the Animal Kingdom. James Nestor, the author, starts the story by sharing the unhealthy progression of his life. He was bottle-fed at six months before he began eating commercial and processed foods. This harmed his health, primarily because of an underdeveloped skull, mouth, and throat.

Centuries now, western medicine has opined that the nose is nothing but an ancillary organ. It can be used for breathing, and when it's blocked, the mouth can take charge of that vital position. Even till now, many scientists, doctors, and researchers still hold on to this assertion. National Institutes of Health has 27 departments that focus only on ears, skin disease, nose, among others but never sinuses and the nose, which is quite unfortunate. Because of this, Jayakar Nayak, a sinus and nasal surgeon, has a reputable laboratory that seeks the hidden knowledge and power of the nose. In one of his studies, he found out that stalactites, marshes, and dunes do many functions for the body. And with this, he believes that we understand little about the nose, hence, why we give credit little importance to it.

Over 40% of the world's population suffers from chronic nasal obstruction. More than half of us have the habit of breathing with our mouths. Of that number, children and females are topping the chart. While this is caused by things like pollution, inflammation allergies, to mention a few. The main reason is the progressively dwindling size of our frontal skull – the nasal cavity.

Small-sized mouths often have their roofs protruding upwards instead of forward to form the high-arched or V-shaped palate. This upward development affects the growth of the nasal cavity, making it small, which consequently impede the delicate nose structures. A congested nasal cavity causes a reduction in airflow, and when that happens, the bacteria in your nostrils flourish, which makes us breathe through the mouth.

Since the dawn of time, humans have been breathing in oxygen, taking advantage of the energy it gives. We were doing this so perfectly before, until 1.5 million years ago, when we had some paradigm shift on how we inhale and exhale. This change was so significant that it affected the way the whole population of humans breathed. From that time, humans began snoring, having a stuffy nose, asthma, wheezing, and allergies. While we think these are all normal since most of us have one of these, the truth is, it is not, and they do not just develop out of the blues. One of the reasons for these issues can be found in our cozy human traits. Standing at the basement of the University of Pennsylvania Museum of Archaeology and Anthropology, James Nestor and Dr. Marianna Evans, a dental researcher, and orthodontist, look at the many skulls of different races, some dating back thousands of years. It was there that Dr. Evans took a skull marked *Parsee* and announced that the jaw and face are twice as large as they are in today's world. She also showed the author the nasal apertures before turning the skull around to show how wide they are.

The doctor and Dr. Kevin Boyd, a college and pediatric dentist in Chicago, has X-trayed over 100 skulls in the Morton Collection, measuring angles from the forehead to the chine and from the ear's top to the nose. The measurements are called the N-perpendicular and Frankfort plane, and they share a striking resemblance to the Parsee's skull we mentioned earlier. These skulls show how humans of centuries ago have a well-proportioned face that would have made breathing very easy for them. They have large mouths complemented with forward facial growth, which make issues like snoring, allergies, wheezing non-existent as they are today. When these ancient skulls are compared with the skulls of their patients, Evans and Boyd found a sharp contrast in their structure. The jaws were receded, the chins had sunken, and the sinuses had wizened. Humans are the only one of all the 5,400 species of mammals to have often overbites, underbites, misshapen teeth, and jaws, as well as malocclusion. This shows instead of passing down our strong traits; we are doing the opposite. The term for this is called "dysevolution". Harvard biologist Daniel Lieberman coined this terminology. It elucidates why we feel aches in our bones. To better understand this, we need to go back in time to when homo sapiens are yet to be that.

Our ancestors started existing 1.7 million years ago as Homo habilis. From there, they foraged for food, built hunting tools, and started grilling and processing food in fire 800,000 years ago. These habits changed our ancestors from the ape-like look to how we look now – the homo Erectus. Our fast-growing skills and knowledge required brain expansion which helped increase in our front face – the location of the mouth, airways, and sinuses. As time goes on, their faces are shortened, with the mouth also shrinking, and we have a protruding nose as opposed to how other uninvolved Homo habilis are. The protruding nose is where our problem began as it became smaller while putting us at risk of airborne bacteria and pathogens.

Three hundred thousand years ago, Homo sapiens egressed from the Africa Savanna alongside other Homos like the Homo heidelbergensis, Homo Naledi and, Homo Neanderthalensis. As time went on, Homo Sapiens discovered speech, which caused the back of the mouth to be broader to allow varying degrees of volumes and utterance. To achieve this, the larynx gets lowered, which makes early humans prone to choking on too big or smaller things that are swallowed wrongly. Sadly, these improvements homo sapiens made in processing food, speech, mastering fire, and expanding the size of our brain, which makes it harder to breathe. However, this didn't cause much issue to these humans until thousands of years later.

Chapter 2: Mouthbreathing

Mouthbreathing is the title given to chapter two of this book. During the halfway mark mouthbreathing phase experiment done by the author and his patient, Olsson. This experiment requires Olsson to come in three times a day to breathe through the mouth while some sensors and thermometers are placed in important places. After this is done, the physiological data is being recorded. The conclusion of the reading shows that breathing through the mouth is doing damage to our health. James' blood pressure spiked to an average of 13 points, putting it in stage one hypertension. Also, his heartbeats variableness dropped sharply, mimicking a body that is in distress. This data is also the same as that of Olsson, and in all, mouthbreathing made them feel awful, which worsens over time.

Additionally, during the experiment, the two of them will take the same set of meals and, number of steps as they check for their blood sugar levels. All these are done while still mouth breathing and doing minimal activities. One day Olsson and James went on a bike ride in the small space of the gym in the neighborhood. The exercise allows them to see the distinction in performance between mouthbreathers and nasal breathers.

The bike experiment isn't something new as it's a repetition of Dr. John Douillard's studies. Douillard is a renowned trainer who trains exclusive athletes. He figured in the 1990s that mouth breathing was harming his clients, and with this discovery, he experimented with professional cyclists riding stationary bikes while he took readings of their heartbeat. Both nasal and mouth breathing were used, and at the end of it all, he discovered that breathing through the nose cut down on force used by 50% while also extending their endurance. The author and Olsson did the same but this time, measuring exertion with distance. The experiment requires them to lock their heart rate to 135 beats per minute with mouth breathing while exercising to know how long they can go. They do this repeatedly for some days before stopping to do the workout again, with nasal breathing. One of the reasons Douillard's experiment was successful is that we take oxygen from the air via aerobic and anaerobic respiration. Anaerobic respiration kicks in when there isn't enough oxygen in the body. It can only be formed from simple sugar, and it is very easy to access, given that it's a backup system. However, energy from anaerobic respiration can be toxic. It creates too much lactic acid, which explains the dizziness, muscle weakness, and even sweat we feel during the first few minutes of working out. However, after our body gets used to it, it switches to aerobic respiration. Phil Maffetone, a reputable fitness coach that had worked with triathletes, Olympians, and ultramarathoners, found out in the 1970s that the majority of the standardized exercises might be causing more harm than good as bodies are not the same. Instead of following this harmful standard, Maffetone made personalized training whose focus is on the metric of heart rates. This allows athletes to stay within the aerobic zone to recover fast while also burning fat more quickly. The best way to find the accurate heart rate for you when exercising is by deducting 180 from your age. The result you get is the highest your body can endure.

Research on mouthbreathing has been going on long before the author and even Douillard. A resourceful doctor in the 1960s by Austen Young's name sewed the nostrils of many chronic nose-bleeders. When Young was no more, Valerie J. Lund, an apprentice of the doctor, resurrected the treatment as she did it for a slew of patients too. The 1970s witnessed Egil P. Harvold's inhumane experiments where he choked up rhesus monkeys' nostrils with silicone. Six months into this, the monkeys began developing negatively. This caused Harvold to repeat the experiment, this time blocking their nostrils for two years. The pictures of these monkeys, even though heart-breaking, showed the sad reality of us humans.

Mouthbreathing negatively changes our body and airways. Mouth inhalation softens the tissues at the back of the mouth, causing it to be loose and move inward to make breathing hard through its constricted look. Nose inhalation, on the other hand, affects the body positively. Air is pushed against soft tissues behind the throat to expand the airways for easy breathing. Because of this, the tissues become "firm" enough to stay in this extended position to continue to make breathing easy. The problem that comes with mouth breathing gets worsened during sleep. Mouthbreathing gets the nostrils blocked, and due to the angles of our heads on the pillow, the airways become even more constricted, which causes sleep apnea and snoring. As the author's experiment goes on, he realizes that his body has begun changing. His throat was closing in, and it felt like he wanted to choke every night. With mouthbreathing, James' snoring rose by 4,820% in just ten days. With up to 25 apnea events because the about 90% drop in oxygen intake level. Breathing through the mouth makes it harder to get to the deepest part of sleep, where a hormone is secreted to prevent hunger, thirst, and even excretion from occurring. One gets severe sleep apnea without having enough deep sleep as the hormone – vasopressin – wasn't secreted.

Contrary to popular beliefs, no amount of snoring is okay. A sleep researcher Dr. Christain Guilleminault discovered that kids who engage in light snoring and do not experience sleep apnea are at higher risk of having blood pressure derangements, mood disorders, learning disabilities, etc. Another Japanese research backed Dr. Guilleminault's research up as rats with blocked nostrils have lower brain cells. They are also twice as long to complete a task than nasal breathing ones. The ancient Chinese put this in perspective as they called mouth *Ni Ch'i,* which translates as adverse breath.

Chapter 3: Nose

Part two of *Breath: The New Science of a Lost Art* is called The Lost Art and Science of Breathing. This also begins with chapter three of the book, which is titled *Nose.* The author noticed a massive difference after the nose plug was pulled from his nostrils to make the end of his mouth breathing experiment. Breathing is more than just allowing air to pass through your nose to provide energy. It exhibits that we have deep connections to the environment and surroundings. The fundamental of respiration is reciprocation. Because of this, the author believes it can lead to restoration. After ten days of mouthbreathing with Olsson, James decides to use the plethora of information, practices, and teachings available to find ways to improve the diaphragm, enlarge the lungs, and increase oxygen intake. In addition to this, he seeks to find a way through the autonomic nervous system while resetting chemo-receptors in the brain to energize immune response.

It is a known fact that the nose is essential as it clear, heats, and moistens it for seamless absorption of air. What, however, is less known is how the nose is also a factor to consider when dealing with issues like erectile dysfunction. The nose has a role in the secretion of chemicals and hormones that make digestion easy and lower blood pressure. In addition, it also influences the stages of women's menstrual cycle, and finally, the mass of your nasal hairs is a great determinant of asthma. Another unknown fact is that the nostrils of humans have their rhythm, which opens and closes according to mental states, mood, and even the moon and the sun.

An ancient Tantric text, the Shiva Swarodaya, 1300 years ago, states that one nostril works while the other rest and vice versa. While one wakes with the sun, the other rises with the moon. In 2004, Dr. Ananda Balayogi Bhavanani, an Indian surgeon, tried to scientifically test this part of the text. While he proved the *Shiva Swarodaya* right, he admitted that the information and reading were anecdotal. However, it is pretty amazing to see that science of centuries ago knew the nostrils' pulse. This is not the only research made on how the nose operates. In 1895 Richard Kayser, a German physician, found out that one of the tissues lining the two nostrils gets congested fast while the other stays open before switching place after 30 minutes to 4 hours. This phenomenon is called the nasal cycle. This cycle is strangely influenced by sexual urges, and this is where things get interesting.

As we have said earlier, that tissue covers the nose's interior. What you didn't know is that this tissue is erectile tissue. The same one is found at the clitoris, penis, and nipples. This, among other things, proves that the nose has more connection to the genitals than we know and even other organs. Even though the nasal cycles had been discovered decades ago, there isn't any good reason to explain why. While many theories are being thrown around, like; it helps protect the nose from respiratory infection or make breathing easier while sleeping, what studies found was totally different. Erectile tissue in the nose has been discovered to mirror the state of one's health. During imbalance or illness, it becomes inflamed, and, nasal cycle happens more when your nose has an infection. The right nostril can be described as a gas pedal because it triggers the "fight or flight" mechanism. Inhaling mainly through this increases your circulation, blood pressure, cortisol levels, and heart rate. Also, it pumps more blood to the prefrontal cortex of your brain associated with language, computing, and logical decision. The left nostril, on the other hand, is the opposite of the right nostril. It serves the function of a brake system for the right nostril. It's pretty connected to the rest-and-relax system as it's intertwined with the parasympathetic nervous system. It also pumps more blood to the prefrontal cortex associated with the production of negative emotions and the formation of mental abstraction

When the breathing of a schizophrenic woman was recorded in 2015 by researchers at the University of California, it was discovered that the left nostril was quite dominant. To operate efficiently, the body needs to be in a state of balance, and this balance can be made possible by the nasal cycle. Nostril breathing, or in yoga term *Nadi Shodhana,* is the act of controlling your body's function through forced breathing via the nostrils.

On the second day of the recovery phase of James' experiment, he breathed through the nostrils. He practiced alternating breathing with his left and right nostrils only to discover it had a tremendously positive effect on his body. His systolic blood pressure reduced from 142 to 124 from the ten days of mouth breathing. His heart variability also jumped up by more than 150%, and he feels less dizzy.

All the component of the nose works together to make you healthy. The turbinates clean, heat, and pressurize air to ensure lungs absorb more oxygen than mouth breathing. The healing powers of the nose surprisingly aren't a new scientific discovery. Around 1,500 BCE, one of the oldest medical texts discovered – Ebers Papyrus – explains that the nostrils are meant for breathing and not the mouth. Even the bible Genesis 2:7 attests to this. But this only got noticed in the 19th century by Geroge Catlin. His adventurous nature helped shed more light on this as he traveled and lived with over 50 different native tribes in America. During all his adventures, he realized that these tribes have almost super-human physical attributes. They are mostly 6 feet tall and above, have a perfectly straight set of teeth, and do not have any form of chronic health issues nor deformities. When asked the secret to this good life, the natives responded by telling him that they breathed. These tribes are known to close kids while sleeping when it's opened, have a good sleeping posture to enhance breathing. Much research was conducted to ensure how vital breathing is, and it all came out positive. This remarkable discovery caused Catlin to publish *The Breath of Life* in 1862, which documents the health benefit of nasal breathing and the health risk of mouthbreathing.

According to Dr. Mark Burhenne, mouth breathing is one of the factors that causes bad breath, periodontal disease, and the leading cause of cavities. Nasal breathing is known to improve nitric oxide by 600%, which explains why we can inhale over 18% than when we practice mouthbreathing. Burhenne uses this nasal breathing technique to cure a five-year-old ADHD and even Ann Kearney, a speech-language pathology at the Stanford Voice and Swallowing Center. She was once a mouthbreather, and it led to tissue blocking her nostrils.

One can practice nasal breathing by consciously and constantly doing it. When you want to sleep, use mouth tape to seal off the mouth when sleeping. All-purpose surgical tape with light adhesive can also work, but the goal remains to seal off the mouth regardless of what you opt for. After practicing breathing through the nostril, Olsson no longer snored, and his apnea even became nonexistent from 53.

Chapter 4: Exhale

Chapter four is titled *Exhale*. As mundane as stretching seems, it is a very ancient and powerful technique that can extend our lung capacity when done consistently. The expansion can go a long way in optimizing our life. The act of stretching has been passed down in secrecy for over 2,500 years by Buddhist monks. Five Tibetan Rites is one of the stretch techniques made famous by Peter Kelder through his booklet The Yes of Revelation. Although Peter might have exaggerated many of his stories, the lung-expanding stretches he talked about were deeply rooted in actual exercises that went back up to 500BCE. These exercises are popular with the Tibetans for millennials as it helps enhance their cardiovascular function, physical fitness, mental health and improve their general well-being in general to give longer life. The Framingham Study gathers data going back to decades of 5,200 subjects to understand the relationship between longevity and lung size. The results they found were terrific. The greatest thing signaling life span is neither diet nor genetics, but the lung capacity.

Subjects with small and less effective lungs get sick faster and are more prone to death. The researchers concluded that the full breaths are measurements of our breathing capacity. Similarly, researchers from the University of Buffalo in 2000 also arrived at the same conclusion after their test. While these studies are correct, they failed to point out that patients with small and deteriorating lungs can improve them while expanding them. The lie we've been made to believe is that we are stuck with whatever lungs we were born with. It's common knowledge that as we grow old, our muscle fibers around the lungs become weak, making it harder to get air in ad the lungs also see a 12% reduction in their size from ages 30-50. This keeps reducing as time goes on and can sometimes get to 30% less, making us susceptible to chronic conditions like anxiety, immune disorders, and high blood pressure. The Tibetans, however, have known one vital thing that western science is only just discovering – aging doesn't necessarily mean declining. Freedivers have been known to expand their lunch capacity up to 40%, and one of the world record holders, Nitsch, is said to have a lung capacity of 14 liters which is twice that of an average man.

Fortunately, deep diving isn't the only way to achieve this. Common exercises like cycling, jogging, or walking have been proven to give up to a 15% increment to one's lung capacity. While Katharina Schroth, a 1990s teenager diagnosed with scoliosis in Dresden, Germany, didn't have this information, she, however, took a cue from the expanding and collapsing of ballons. She would twist her body and breathe multiple times in a day using different methods. In just five years of doing this, she was able to cure herself of this condition. In other words, she breathes her curved spine to health. This colossal breakthrough made her share her technique with other scoliosis patients. They were all cured through breathing and stretching. Even with her successful track record, the medical community fought her, claiming she had no qualification for all that she was doing. But that didn't hinder the progress and restoration she was giving to these otherwise helpless patients. She went on to do this for 60 years of her life till she was given the Federal Cross of Merit award by the German government for the pacesetting discovery and innovation.

During the research for this book, Nestor went to Lynn Martin, a breathing expert, to find different ways to expand their lungs. They talked about Carl Stough, one of the first few people who understand the power of breathing in the western world. Although Stough didn't become famous, nor did his discoveries, his findings are undoubtedly outstanding. One of the lost secrets discovered by Stough was that breathing is more than just inhalation and exhalation. Instead, effective breathing and increasing lung capacity can only be achieved through full exhalation. Through this, he made his singers in Westminister Choir College sing clearer by expanding their lungs through breathing. His success brought him out to the world, and he was asked by Dr. Maurice J. Small, the chief of tuberculosis management, in 1958 to train a new group of people who couldn't sing. On getting there, he realized his new students were patients with emphysema. This seemed like a big problem at first but was able to correct the damaged diaphragm of these elderly patients gradually that they were able to say a full sentence in a single breath. The before and after x-ray of these patients shows immense improvement, and even though Stough didn't find a cure to emphysema, as damage done to the lung is irreversible, he was able to discover how to access the still functional part of it. In the next decade, he treated more patients in VA hospitals and even expanded the treatments to patients with pneumonia, asthma, and bronchitis. Stough; Dr. Breathe went ahead to train people to help fight respiratory weakness and improve their state of well-being by breathing effectively. Stough trained the U.S men's team for the 1968 Olympics in Mexico City. They could win 12 Olympic medals consisting of 5 world records, and most of the medals were gold.

Even though Martin worked as an associate with Stough for over two decades, he didn't let her in on his secrets as he couldn't find the right way to convey his message. There is only one footage of him in the 1992 Aspen Music Festival showing what he did and how he was able to do it.

Sadly, with all the progress Stough made, no one talked or implemented any of his findings. Until today, Emphysema and many conditions reversed through breathing and enlarging the lungs are still listed as uncurable.

Chapter 5: Slow

Chapter five is titled "Slow." The author had not trusted Olsson when he first interviewed him more than a year ago. That was mainly because Olsson had mentioned that toxic gas could work restorative wonders. Olsson had even said that carbon dioxide was more important than oxygen and that it was carbon dioxide, not oxygen, that fostered the burst of life 500 million years ago.

At a point, the author thought that Olsson was either nuts or just good with exaggerations. Everything Olsson had said went against what the author knew. Carbon dioxide was a waste metabolic product that we were supposed to get out of our system.

After a series of arguments with Olsson, the author decided to fly to Sweden and spend a few days with Olsson to know more about one of the most misunderstood gases in the universe. When they met, Olsson told him his story. Olsson's father had died of lung disease and high blood pressure at 68. Knowing there were chances that he would end up like his dad, Olsson sold his business, got divorced, downsized, and began to research the history of health, medicine, and the role that breathing and carbon dioxide played in the body. Olsson found that the most efficient way to prevent chronic health problems, increase longevity, and improve athletic performance is to focus on how we breathe and then balance oxygen and carbon dioxide. To do this, we need to learn how to inhale and exhale slowly.

To understand how breathing less is more beneficial, we need to first understand how the body structures work.

Every breath we take goes from the throat throughout the body until oxygen disembarks, fueling hungry cells. Carbon dioxide would get on board and get out through the nose and mouth.

For every ten pounds of fat that we lose, eight and a half of it comes out through the lungs, not sweat or urine. The lungs are the body's weight-regulating system, and what our bodies need to function properly is not more oxygen but more carbon dioxide.

A Danish physiologist, Christian Bohr, discovered this when he experimented on pigs, chickens, and other animals. He found that when animals breathed less, they would produce more energy, and when they breathed heavily and more rapidly, the blood flow to their tissues, muscles, and organs would reduce.

Yandell Henderson, the director of the Laboratory of Applied Psychology at Yale, began to experiment with carbon dioxide and metabolism years after Bohr published a paper on the study. According to Yandell, over-breathing has no benefit to tissue, and it can cause a case of oxygen deficiency that can lead to relative suffocation. To prove his point, he conducted an awful experiment on some dogs. He pumped some dogs with a large amount of air that made their heartbeat rate jump from 40 to 200 per minute. The oxygen in these dogs would be too much, and they would have minimal carbon dioxide to offload, causing the dogs' tissues and organs to fail. The dogs would often go into a coma, and if he continued, they would eventually die.

When he made dogs breathe slightly harder than normal, they would show symptoms during panic attacks or altitude sickness. To slow their heart rates back to normal, he would administer morphine and other drugs, which worked because they raised carbon dioxide levels.

However, there is another used by Henderson to slow the dogs' heartbeat rate by letting them breathe slowly. According to Henderson, Carbon dioxide is a more fundamental component of living matter than oxygen.

By the end of the author's trip to Olsson, he had understood why the man had left everything and immersed himself in the knowledge of breathing techniques and carbon dioxide. They kept in touch after Olsson returned home, and that was how Olsson ended up in the author's living room.

Olsson took very slow breaths, three times slower than the average American, which made his rise by 25 percent while his blood pressure and heart rate dropped. His oxygen, on the other hand, stayed the same. This is because when we breathe at a normal rate, our lungs will absorb only a quarter of the available oxygen while the rest is exhaled right back. This means that when we take long breathes, we are allowing our lungs to soak up mire in fewer breaths

The next day, on his ride, the author began to experiment with his breathing, and he soon realized that his oxygen hadn't decreased with these slow breaths; instead, the levels rose.

It has also been discovered that a form of slow breathing occurs when we pray. In an experiment conducted by researchers at the University of Pavia in Italy, subjects were asked to recite the Buddhist mantra and the original

Latin version of the rosary, the Ave Maria, that priests and the congregation recite.

What they discovered was that the average number of breaths for each cycle was almost identical. Whenever they follow this breathing pattern, the blood flow to the brain increases, and the function of the heart, nervous system, and circulation falls into place. When the subjects went back to spontaneous breathing and talking, their heart would beat erratically, and the integration of their system would fall apart.

Chapter 6: Less

Chapter six is titled "Less." The average American BMI (Body Mass Index) increased by 38% in just 50 years, and one in three persons in the United States of America are untamed. It is harder to calculate the breathing rate these days, but the few available studies paint a troubling picture.

Our culture overeats, which has also affected how we breathe, as a quarter of the population presently suffers from chronic over-breathing.

While the solution is to breathe less, it isn't as easy as it sounds. However, with training and efforts, we can cultivate the habit of breathing less.

Indian yogis, Chinese doctors, and Tibetan Buddhists have all perfected the art of breathing less. Now breathing less is not the same as breathing slower, but there are a lot of benefits that come with fewer inhales and smaller amounts of exhales. The goal is to breathe less.

By the end of the author's Stanford experiment, he began to see the immense benefits of slowing his breathing rate. His blood pressure dropped, the variability of his heart rate rose, and he became more energetic.

Olsson encouraged the author to jog while also practicing breathing even less. Each breath they take should be about three seconds, while each breath out should take four seconds. Now, the inhales will remain the same while the exhales move up to five, six, and even seven seconds during the run.

When you take slower and longer exhales, your carbon dioxide level increases, and with those extra carbon dioxides, you gain a higher aerobic endurance. When you train your body to breathe less, your VO2 max increases which, in turn, increases your athletic stamina and helps you live a longer and healthier life.

The pioneer of less is more is Konstantin Pavlovich Buteyko, a mechanic turned Medical student who began to research "Man" after the end of the World War. During his residency rounds, he realized that patients in worse health seemed to breathe far too much.

He suffered from severe high blood pressure, headaches, stomach pains, and heart pain. By 29, his systolic blood pressure had shot high, and the Doctors told him he had a year to live. One night during his shift, Buteyko made a discovery. He realized that his symptoms reduced drastically when he took fewer breaths. He shared this with an asthma patient who was in the middle of an asthmatic attack. After some careful breath, the attack disappeared.

While the author took the jog with Olsson, they practiced an extreme version of Buteyko's techniques on himself. This technique involved limiting their inhales and extending their exhales past their comfort zones. The purpose of this exercise was to make the body comfortable with a high amount of carbon dioxide, and this will, in turn, make their body breathe less during their restring hours or the next time they workout.

Buteyko moved in the late 50s and moved to Akademgorodok, a research facility in central Siberia. There, he conducted an experiment involving more than

200 researchers and assistants. The experiment showed that sick subjects with diseases like asthma, hypertension, etc., breathed pretty much the same while the healthy subjects also breathed alike. The sick subjects take 15 or more liters of air per minute, and the healthy ones only take five to six liters of air.

The subjects practiced the technique, and the sick ones had reports of better health while the healthy ones felt even better. Also, subjects who were athletes recorded better performances.

Around this time, there was a five-foot, and eight inches man in the town of Zlin named Zatopek. He took athleticism seriously when he came second after being elected to participate in a local race. He developed a training method that gave him an edge: running as fast as possible while holding his breath.

Even though people mocked Zatopek's training method, he ignored them and went ahead to win several awards, even breaking the country's national records. He also won the Olympic gold medal in 1952 and went ahead to get named "The Greatest Runner of All Time" by Runner's World Magazine.

After Zatopek, the hypoventilation training didn't quite pick up as many athletes steered clear of it due to how uncomfortable it was. Decades later, however, a swim coach in the United States, James Counsilman, rediscovered the technique. While regular swimmers take three-stroke before they flip their head to the side and inhale, Counsilman trained his team to hold their breath for as long as nine strokes. His team went ahead to win13 gold medals, 14 silver, and seven bronze, setting a world record in eleven events.

The technique, once again, fell into obscurity when several studies argued that the technique had little to no impact on the performance of the athletes. Decades later, however, Dr. Xavier Woorons found that these studies were flawed. His research and report proved that hypoventilation boosts the red blood cell and this, in turn, allows the athlete to carry more oxygen and produce more energy with each breath.

Aside from athletes, the average person gains a lot from this training as a few weeks of it increased endurance and reduced "trunk fat," among other things.

During the author's run with Olsson, he finds the extended technique suggested by Olsson incredibly laborious, and he soon settled for one that was more tolerable. A few minutes later, the author began to sense an intense heat at the back of his neck and pixelated vision. This was the good headache that Olsson was talking about, and it was a result of carbon dioxide increasing and oxygen dislodging from the hemoglobin. The jog ended before he could reach some existential crescendo, but the jog proved to him that there was a lot to gain from the "less" approach.

Throughout his career, Buteyko faced criticism and even suffered physical attacks with his laboratory also getting burnt, but all these were not enough to stop him. In the 1980s, his technique was recognized by the Soviet Ministry of Health as effective. He also met with Prince Charles, who he helped heal from breathing difficulties.

Before Buteyko started his treatments, asthma had become a global epidemic, and even now, 8 percent of the population in America suffer from it. Asthma can be brought on by over-breathing and asthmatic people as a whole breath more than the regular person. Many people living with asthma have taught themselves the technique of breathing less, and they have reported dramatic results.

Chapter 7: Chew

Chapter seven is titled "Chew." On the nineteenth day of the Standford experiment, the author reduced his blood pressure by 20 points, and his carbon dioxide level had risen consistently. He was able to achieve all these by breathing slowly through his nose.

The catalyst to writing this book was a mundane act that was the few seconds of soft chewing.

Twelve centuries ago, the humans in South-West Asia and the Fertile Crescent in the Eastern Mediterranean began to grow their food. That was when they began to suffer a series of crooked teeth and deformed mouths. Three hundred years later, these deformities became viral throughout the world. The industrialization of farmed food caused humans to be one of the worst breathers in the animal kingdom.

Because this type of research hasn't been made in the medical field, the author had to acquaint himself with anthropologists working in ancient burial sites. The author traveled to Paris, and there, he saw a stack of human bones.

By 1500, food became more processed, and these lacked the necessary fiber and the full nutrients that humans need. This caused the urban population to go sick, resulting in a rise in the mortality rate. The average human became shorter and the human face deteriorated.

In Paris, he saw human skulls and bones of the Patient Zeros of the modern Industrial mouth. The symmetry of their faces was different, and their skull looked lopsided.

Researchers suspect that the industrialization of food has destroyed our breathing and has caused our mouths to shrink. In 1930, it was decided that the culprit was not the lack of one Vitamin but the deficiency of all of them.

This was discovered by research conducted by Weston Price confirmed. The research showed that communities eating traditional food had better teeth, general health, and airways than the urban humans that ate industrialized food, and this was because the rural people had diets that contained vitamins and minerals.

Price was only partly right because the problem wasn't just what they ate; it was how they ate it. What was lacking from our diet was chewing. Our ancestors chewed for hours long, and this was why their throats, teeth, mouth, and faces were so strong and wide.

The author left Paris on a bad note because he realized that industrialization – that was supposed to help – actually had damning consequences. He realized that breathing less, slow, and exhaling deeply wouldn't matter much if we could not get our breaths down because of our small mouths and caved-in faces. The author began to seek solutions to this problem.

A doctor that the author met told him that the surgery that corrects chronic sinusitis was usually successful. However, a few percentages of patients end up having more than necessary tissue removed from their noses. These unfortunate patients end up with a condition called "empty nose syndrome," which causes them to take in more air, making them even more breathless and anxious.

Thicker necks, deeper uvula, teeth that overlap the molar, and thicker necks are all obstacles contributing to the mouth's obstruction.

One of the ways to treat airway obstruction is by continuously using a positive airway pressure mask or CPAP as it forces bursts of air past the obstructed airway.

Dentists, over the years, have worked on widening mouths and opening airways, and they have been designing different devices to help with this right from the mid-1800s. These devices require maintenance, and they can be very uncomfortable to wear. By the 1940s, people had multiple teeth extracted, but this didn't help because removing teeth would only make a small mouth even smaller. The devices founded by traditional orthodontists were found to make the mouth smaller and worsen breathing.

Mike, a dentist, said that the first step to dealing with airway obstruction wasn't orthodontists but maintaining correct "oral posture." Our body hates bad postures, and it triggers a lot of neurological problems.

Mike also suggests another exercise called "mewing," which involves pushing the back of the tongue against the back roof of the mouth then moving the rest of the tongue forward until the tip of the tongue hits the back of the front teeth.

The author also visited Dr. Theodore Belfor, a dentist who was introduced to a device that looked like an old monobloc that helped chronic snorers sleep peacefully and aided opera singers in hitting even higher notes. It also straightened the teeth and aided breathing.

The more we chew, the more stem cells we release. This triggers more bone density and growth so that we look younger and breathe better.

Belfor used a mold to fit the author with a Homeoblock, an expanding device invented in the 1990s. Its functions are to expand the mouth, stimulate the stress of chewing and breathing better.

Whenever humans or animals shifted from harder food to softer ones, their faces would narrow, their teeth would crowd, and their jaws would fall out of alignment, and all these trigger breathing problems. The official website of the US National Institutes of Health did not acknowledge this as a cause of airway blockage.

Belfor had data to prove his argument, but his studies were shunned and ridiculed. About a year after the author began to wear Belfor's retainer, he visited a radiology clinic where results showed that he had gained more than a thousand cubic millimeters of new bones in his cheeks. Other parts of his face also recorded improvements in his eyes, nose, jaw, and airway.

Chapter 8: More on Occasion

Chapter eight is titled "More on Occasion." The study ended, and Olsson and the author departed after being told that the result would be out in about a month. The author went ahead to pursue other techniques that were not the slow and less method. The author calls these techniques Breathing+, and they can radically transform lives if practiced willingly. Some of these techniques involve breathing fast, while some have to do with breathing slow. With some techniques, you don't even have to breathe at all for some minutes.

The Breathing+ technique was started during the Civil War when several soldiers suffered from "Irritable Heart Syndrome," which affected their heartbeat and digestive system. Da Costa, the physician who treated them then, called the condition "a disorder of the sympathetic nervous system," This was what the author was currently feeling.

The author had hired someone to help him redline his sympathetic nervous system with over-breathing, and it was working.

There are two sections of our autonomic nervous system; the first is parasympathetic that stimulates feel-good hormones, and opens the floodgates of tears when we are in emotional states. The other, the sympathetic section, is the one that sends signals to our organs to get ready for action when there is an emergency. The sympathetic section only gets triggered occasionally, and while it takes seconds to turn it on, it would take hours to switch it off and for the body to get back to a state of relaxation.

Now, ancients developed a breathing technique that puts them under an extended state of this sympathetic stress every day.

The author was practicing one of the techniques called "Inner Fire Meditation." This method was founded when a 28-year-old Indian called Naropa harnessed the power of his breath to keep himself from freezing to death in a cold cave. This technique, "Tummo," which means "inner fire," is dangerous and can cause severe mental harm if misused.

The soldiers that Da Costa treated experienced unconscious stress, which was caused by the carnages they saw that triggered their unconscious sympathetic responses. The fact that they had no means of releasing this stress made their nervous system overloaded, and they ended up shortcutting and collapsing.

Professional surfers, martial arts fighters, and even the Navy SEALs use the Tunmo-style breathing. It is also beneficial to middle-aged people who suffer from aches and pain. For the author, Tunmo was a preventative measure to get his fraying nervous system on track. What Tummo does is give the body a violent shove it needs to get realigned.

Dr. Stepehn Porges, a scientist, studied the nervous system for years, primarily focusing on the vagus, a powerful lever that turns the body on or off in response to stress. The vagus nerve slows the heart rate, circulation, and organ functions when it perceives high-stress levels. The vagus nerve is in charge of fainting, and while some humans are oversensitive that seeing a spider can cause them to faint, most of us who aren't that sensitive would also be unable to relax; suspended in the space of half-anxiety. In this state, our bodies can keep us alive but not healthy because the communication between the organ and the brain is choppy.

In the past decade, surgeons have treated the Costa-like maladies with implanted electrical nodes that work as an artificial vagal nerve that restarts organ communication and blood flow in patients. The procedure is called vagus nerve stimulation.

Porges, however, found a less invasive way to stimulate the vagus nerve, and that is by breathing. Breathing slowly will open up the communication of the vagal network, thereby getting us into a parasympathetic state.

This is supposed to be biologically impossible, especially since the nervous system is supposed to be automatic.

A Harvard Medical school researcher, Herbert Benson, after hearing different stories of the wonders of Tummo, flew to the Himalayas and conducted an experiment during which the body temperature of monks who practiced Tummo increased to as much as 17 Fahrenheit. The result of this was published in the scientific journal "Nature" the following year. In the early 2000s, a Dutchman, Wim Hof, performed a series of feats that were supposed to be impossible after discovering Tummo. Researchers at Radboud University researched a dozen of healthy male volunteers within ten days. Those who were taught Tummo could control their heart rate, immune response, temperature, and even stimulate their sympathetic system.

Like the author's cheerleader McGee, 15% of the American population suffers from an autoimmune disorder. The medications prescribed for these conditions usually would only suppress the condition, not eliminate it. McGee, however, became introduced to the Wim Hof heavy breathing technique, and he recorded drastic positive results.

Aside from Tummo, another heavy breathing technique called Holotropic Breathwork was created by a Czech psychiatrist called Stanislav Grof. This technique was more or less Tummo raised to power 11. For this technique, you have to breathe hard and quick to the point of exhaustion so that they would get to the point of stress before returning to a state of groovy calm.

A psychiatrist, Dr. James Eyerman, used this technique to treat patients for 30 years, which yielded life-changing results. The author decided to sign up for a session where he witnessed people react to the technique. At the end of the session, he wondered if the curative effects of the technique were a result of the environment and setting and how much of it was due to breathing heavily for a long time.

The blood flow in the brain usually stays consistent – altering a little during exercise – but when we breathe heavily, the brain blood flow can decrease by 40 percent. This explains why a lot of people experience sensations of death during Holotropic Breathwork

Chapter 9: Hold It

Chapter nine is titled "Hold It." In 1968, Dr. Arthur Kling experimented on monkeys, removing their amygdalae and two almond-sized nodes at the center of their temporal lobe and then releasing them into the forest where they all died because they could no longer recognize danger or fear.

A lady, S.M., suffers from a condition that destroyed her amygdalae. This caused her to have no sense of fear, danger, hunger, and she would even, sometimes, go off with strangers. Dr. Justin Feinstein worked with her for decades, and nothing he did or showed her ever scared her. There was a breakthrough when he administered carbon dioxide to her as she was thrown into a state of panic.

This proves that the amygdalae are not the only "alarm circuit of fear" and that there is another, which is the fear that comes from being unable to breathe.

When we breathe too slowly, our carbon-dioxide level will rise, and the central chemoreceptors would send alarm signals to the brain to tell us to breathe faster and more deeply. The central chemoreceptor would also tell our brain to breathe slower when we breathe too fast, and our carbon dioxide level decreases.

We can, however, train our chemoreceptors to adapt to be flexible, so it doesn't react when we reach physical or mental limits. 18% of the American population suffer from a form of anxiety, and perhaps, this can be treated by conditioning the central chemoreceptors and the other parts of the brain to be more flexible to the levels of carbon dioxide.

In ancient India, they practiced a breathing technique that means "trance induced by stopping all breathing," Yet today, breath-holding is associated with the disease. In fact, a chronic unconscious breath-holding condition called sleep apnea is damaging, and it is the same with another condition called "email apnea." The difference between the ancient breathing technique and these conditions is will. The former is conscious, while the latter is unconscious.

Feinstein got an NIH grant, and he used it to test the use of inhaled carbon dioxide on patients who suffer from panic and anxiety disorder. His therapy didn't require that the patients hold their breath or anything; all they had to do was inhale carbon dioxide and flex their chemoreceptors back to normal.

This carbon dioxide therapy has been around for centuries, and it yielded tremendous results until scientific research suddenly disappeared in the 1950s. More than half of the American population will suffer from either depression or anxiety in their lifetime, and while there are treatments, most of these treatments are not without flaws. Breathing, on the other hand, is available to everyone.

In a controlled trial, Alicia Meuret, a psychologist at the Southern Methodist University, helped patients blunt asthma attacks by slowing their breathing to increase their carbon dioxide. This method also works for panic attacks.

The author decided to experience Feinstein's carbon dioxide technique, and right before the procedure started, he remembered the first time he visited Olsson in Stockholm. Olsson had taken the author to his office, where the author was shown results of some experiments carried out by a group of DIY pulmonaut. This experiment had to do with mixing 7 percent of carbon dioxide into the room air. It offered potent results, with most of the users reporting incredible effects.

Back in Feinstein's office, the author was strapped in and inhaled the carbon dioxide. He did not feel anything at first, but that was because he was already used to the Wim Hof technique. Soon enough, he began to feel like he had a sock jammed in his mouth that was restricting his airflow. It was over soon, and he could suddenly breathe again. He did it over and over again. It was a form of exposure therapy, and the more he exposed himself to the gas, the more flexible his chemoreceptor would be.

Chapter 10: Fast, Slow, and not at all

Chapter ten is titled "Fast, Slow, and not at all." The author went to Sao Paulo, Brazil, to see a renowned expert in foundations of yoga called Luiz Sergio Alvares DeRose. The author came to this man because he had a lot of questions like why the body heats up during Tummo, why the monks who practice a softer version of Tummo can be alive and healthy even after reducing their metabolic rates by as much as 64 percent when they should have either been dead or suffering from severe hypothermia. Another question was how Breathing+ techniques like Holotropic Breathwork could induce hallucinatory and hyper surreal effects on people.

The author went to DeRose because he believes that the man has the answers to his questions; after all, DeRose has written 30 books about the oldest forms of yoga and breathing. He has received several awards reserved for great states people.

Prana is a commonly used word in yoga, and it means "life force" or "vital energy" and this term is an ancient theory of atoms that says that everything is made of swirling bits of atoms, and the more prana something has, the more alive it is. In China, it is called "ch'i," and in Japan, it is called "ki."

Several methods are used to open up prana channels and distribute the energy, but the most powerful is to inhale prana. When we breathe, we expand our life source.

Western science never really observed prana until they examined Swami Rama, a yoga and breathing techniques teacher. During this examination, Rama placed himself under a "yogic sleep" that made his brain go to sleep while his mind was active. The EEG read Rama to be deep asleep, but when he woke up, he gave a detailed recap of everything that had been said while his brain displayed waves of deep sleep.

In another experiment, Rama slowed down his heart and then made his heart rate go down to zero, staying in this state for 30 seconds. This state was supposed to have resulted in cardiac arrest, but Rama was unaffected. In fact, he said he could remain in this state for half an hour. The result of this experiment was reported in New York Times.

He could do this with some strange prana force, but the team could not calculate it with any of their machines.

Rama soon became a superstar, but in reality, Rama wasn't the first person to have done this. In fact, a French cardiologist called Therese Brosse had recorded a yogi doing the same thing forty years ago. While Rama revealed some of his secrets in group lessons and videos, he never really elaborated on them.

The best explanation on the "vital substance" of prana that the author got came from a Hungarian scientist, Albert Szent-Gyorgyi. Szent-Gyorgyi wanted to understand the process of breathing and how the breath we take interacts with our tissues, muscles, and organs on a subatomic level. He wanted to know how life gained energy from the air.

All matter is energy at its most basic level, and the only thing that distinguishes inanimate objects from animate ones is the level of energy.

Szent-Gyorgyi studied the earliest forms of life that were "weak electron acceptors" that couldn't take in or release electrons. They soon evolved and began to consume oxygen quickly. The surplus energy led to the early life evolving to plants, insects, and everything else.

It is the same with life today; the more oxygen life consumes, the more animated it becomes. The living matter remains healthy when it can absorb and transfer oxygen in a controlled way. On the other hand, when cell matters lose the ability to offload and absorb electrons, they begin to break down. In humans, this leads to cancer, which is one reason cancer develops and thrives in an environment with low oxygen.

The most effective way to keep our tissues healthy is by mimicking the reactions that evolved in early aerobic life on Earth; that is, making our bodies a "strong electron acceptor." This can be achieved by breathing slow and less through the nose to balance the levels of the respiratory gases in the body.

With the local tradition in every culture, healing has been accomplished by moving energy. In fact, the moving energy of electrons allows living things to stay healthy and alive for as long as possible.

Szent-Gyorgyi died at the ripe age of 93.

Five thousand years ago, where we now have the border of Afghanistan, there existed the Indus-Sarasvati civilization. The people did not believe in any God or religion. Instead, they believed in the transformative power of breathing.

This was the birthplace of yoga. Around 2000 BCE, a drought hit, and the Aryans from the northwest moved to the land, taking their culture, rewriting and condensing it in their native language of Sanskrit. It spread, and by 500 BCE, the techniques had been synthesized into the yoga sutras of Patanjali.

In the Yoga Sutra, there is no mention of moving or repeating poses. It was about sitting and holding the breath still to build prana through breathing.

This was the kind of ancient yoga DeRose tasted in the 1970s. Unlike the hybridized yoga being practiced today, what DeRose learned was the one that first originated 5,000 years ago.

According to DeRose, yoga was not designed to cure problems. Instead, it was designed to make healthy people reach their full potential, to give them the conscious power to heat themselves on demand, control their nervous systems and hearts, expand their consciousness, and overall, live a longer and more vibrant life.

The author told DeRose about his experience in the Victorian house ten years ago and how he had been floored while practicing the ancient pranayama technique called Sudarshan. He also told him about how a milder version of the same reaction happened to himself and million others when they used traditional yogic breathing.

DeRose responded by telling the author that it was all energy. His explanation was that author had built up too much prana breathing so heavily for so long, but he hadn't yet adapted to it. According to DeRose, Sudarshan meant "good vision," which was precisely what the author had experienced.

The key to Tummo, Sudarshan Kriya, and the other breathing techniques is to be patient, maintain flexibility, and slowly absorb what breathing offers.
Before the author left Brazil, his translator, Pinhero, taught him some of the ancient techniques that DeRose is known for.

Background Information about *Breath*

The book, Breathe, was released on May 26, 2020 through Riverhead/Penguin Random House. It shines a light on how humans have lost the ability to breathe over the past centuries. This has caused us to suffer from a variety of ailments like sleep apnea, snoring, autoimmune disease and several others.

To write this book, the author travels around the world to learn more about how and where we went wrong as humans, and more importantly, what we can do to fix that. In this book, James Nestor has to draw on a millennium of studies in psychology, human physiology, pulmonology and biochemistry.

Background Information about James Nestor

James Nestor is a journalist and an author and he has written for Outside Magazine, National Public Radio, Dwell Magazine, The New York Times, Scientific America and more.

His first book, DEEP, was released in 2014 and it made BBC Book of the Week. The book also got nominated for several awards like PEN American Center Best Sports Book of the Year, an Amazon Best Science Book of 2014, BuzzFeed 19 Best Nonfiction Books of 2014, among others.

He has presented his research at several institutions like the United Nations, UBS, Stanford Medical school, and Global Classroom (World Health Organization+UNICEF). He has also featured on more than 40 television and radio shows.

Awards & Accolades

1. Worked for Outside Magazine, The Atlantic, National Public Radio, The New York Times and a lot more.

2. Authored a New York Times bestseller.

3. Presented at Stanford Medical School, the United Nations, UBS, Global Classroom (World Health Organization+UNICEF).

Trivia Questions

1. Is the author able to convince you of his point?
2. Is there enough evidence given to back up the author's claim?
3. Where does man's breathing problem seem to come from?
4. How helpful is stretching?

Trivia Questions About Breath

1. What was the author's thought the first time he interviewed Olsson?
2. What are the two types of respiration?
3. Which part of the brain does the left nostril stimulate?
4. Which part of the brain does the right nostril stimulate?
5. What are the disadvantages of mouth breathing?
6. What seems to be the leading cause of mouth breathing?
7. What was the result of Yendell Henderson's experiment?
8. Who is the pioneer of less is more?
9. How did Zatopek perform his athletic feat?
10. What was the outcome of the industrialization of food?
11. What causes empty nose syndrome?
12. What does the sympathetic section of the autonomic nervous system do?
13. What less invasive way to stimulate the vagus nerve did Porges find?
14. What happens when someone's amygdalae gets destroyed?
15. What did the author feel when he inhaled the carbon dioxide?
16. Who did the author travel to see in Brazil?
17. How was Rama able to slow his heart?

Trivia Questions About James Nestor

1. What magazine has James Nestor worked for?
2. When did James Nestor release DEEP?
3. When was Breathe released?

More books from Smart Reads

Thank You

Hope you've enjoyed your reading experience.

We here at Smart Reads will always strive to deliver to you the highest quality guides.

So I'd like to thank you for supporting us and reading until the very end.

Before you go, would you mind leaving us a review on Amazon?

It will mean a lot to us and support us creating high quality guides for you in the future.

Thanks once again!

Warmly yours,

The Smart Reads Team

Download Your Free Gift

As a way to say "Thank You" for being a fan of our series,
I've included a free gift for you:

Brain Health: How to Nurture and Nourish Your Brain For
Top Performance

Go to www.smart-reads.com to get your
FREE book.

The Smart Reads Team